• WEIRD SPACE SC

SPACE JUNK

THE BREAKDOWN

VIRGINIA LOH-HAGAN

45TH PARALLEL PRESS

Published in the United States of America by Cherry Lake Publishing Group
Ann Arbor, Michigan
www.cherrylakepublishing.com

Photo Credits: © janiecbros/iStock, cover, 1, 10-11; © VectorMine /Adobe Stock, 7; © Dima Zel/Shutterstock, 8; © Artsiom P/Shutterstock, 13; © Gorodenkoff/Shutterstock, 15; © The Stock Image Bank /Adobe Stock, 18; © Framestock /Adobe Stock, 20-21

Graphic Element Credits: Cover, multiple interior pages: © WindAwake/Shutterstock, © kichikimi/Shutterstock, © Your Local Llamacorn/Shutterstock, © Marishiav/Shutterstock, © Supza/Shutterstock, © HSSstudio/Shutterstock, © Olive Kitt/Shutterstock, © KKarance/Shutterstock, © Theo_hrm/Shutterstock, © Rodin Anton/Shutterstock, © Petr Vaclavek/Shutterstock, © Nikolaeva/Shutterstock, © Evgenii Doljenkov/Shutterstock

45th Parallel Press is an imprint of Cherry Lake Publishing Group.

Library of Congress Cataloging-in-Publication Data has been filed and is available at catalog.loc.gov

Cherry Lake Publishing Group would like to acknowledge the work of the Partnership for 21st Century Learning, a Network of Battelle for Kids. Please visite Battelle for Kids online for more information.

Printed in the United States of America

Dr. Virginia Loh-Hagan is an author, university professor, and former classroom teacher. She's currently the Director of the Asian Pacific Islander Desi American Resource Center at San Diego State University. She loves science-fiction stories. She lives in San Diego with her very tall husband and very naughty dogs.

TABLE OF CONTENTS

BREAK IT DOWN

1. DECODE IT

- Look at each letter.
- Look at letter patterns.
- Blend sounds.
- Try other possible sounds.

2. BUILD VOCABULARY

- Listen to the word.
- Match the sounds to a word you know.
- Look for context clues for words you don't know.
- Look up the meaning in a glossary or dictionary.

3. MAKE CONNECTIONS

- Name other examples.
- Draw the idea.
- Compare ideas.
- Ask questions.

TEST IT OUT

WORDS YOU'LL LEARN

Look over the list of vocabulary words. Are there any you already know?

debris
innovative
monitor
orbits
spacecraft
twilight
vehicles

GET STARTED

Many words have silent letters. Silent letters often have patterns. They may be letters that were pronounced long ago. They may be spelling patterns from other languages.

- Look at the letters.
- Chunk long words to read them.
- Try long and short vowel sounds.
- Try ignoring letters that sound out of place.

The word *debris* has French roots. The *s* is silent. It is pronounced: duh-BREE.

- The 1st vowel says "uh": *duh-*.
- The 2nd vowel is a long *e*: *-bree*.

What do you think happens to trash in space?

It becomes **debris**. This means pieces of waste.

BUILD VOCABULARY

Debris (duh-BREE) is what is left. It is left when a thing breaks. It is pieces of waste.

- Most debris doesn't break down. It stays. It pollutes.
- Other phrases: plant debris, falling debris, piece of debris

Trash in space can come from space objects.

It can come from human-made objects.

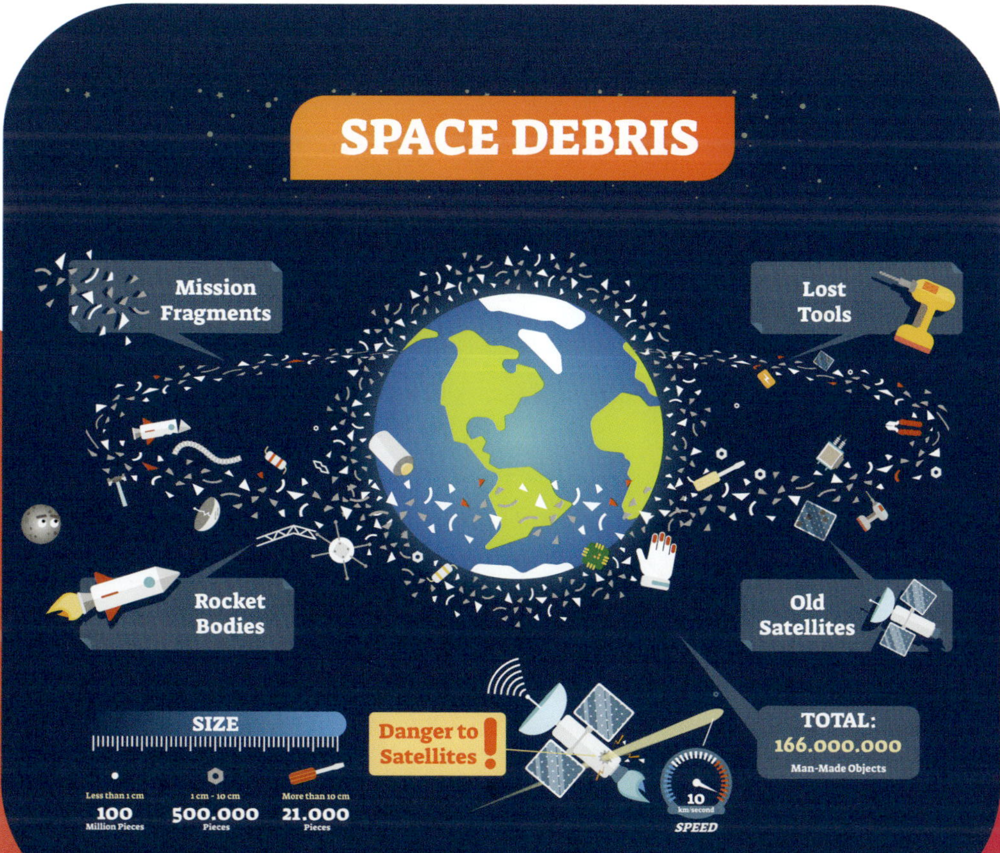

Human trash includes broken **spacecraft** parts.

It includes paint chips from rockets.

Spacecrafts are **vehicles** used to travel in space. A vehicle carries or moves people or things.

DECODE IT

The word *vehicle* has a silent letter.

- Break it into chunks: ve-hi-cle.
- The "h" is silent in this word.
- The 1st vowel sound is a long *e*.
- The middle and last vowel sounds say "uh."
- *Vehicle* is pronounced VEE-uh-kuhl.

Over 100 million pieces of space junk circle Earth.

More space junk means more danger.

Space junk can travel up to 17,500 miles (28,163.5 kilometers) per hour.

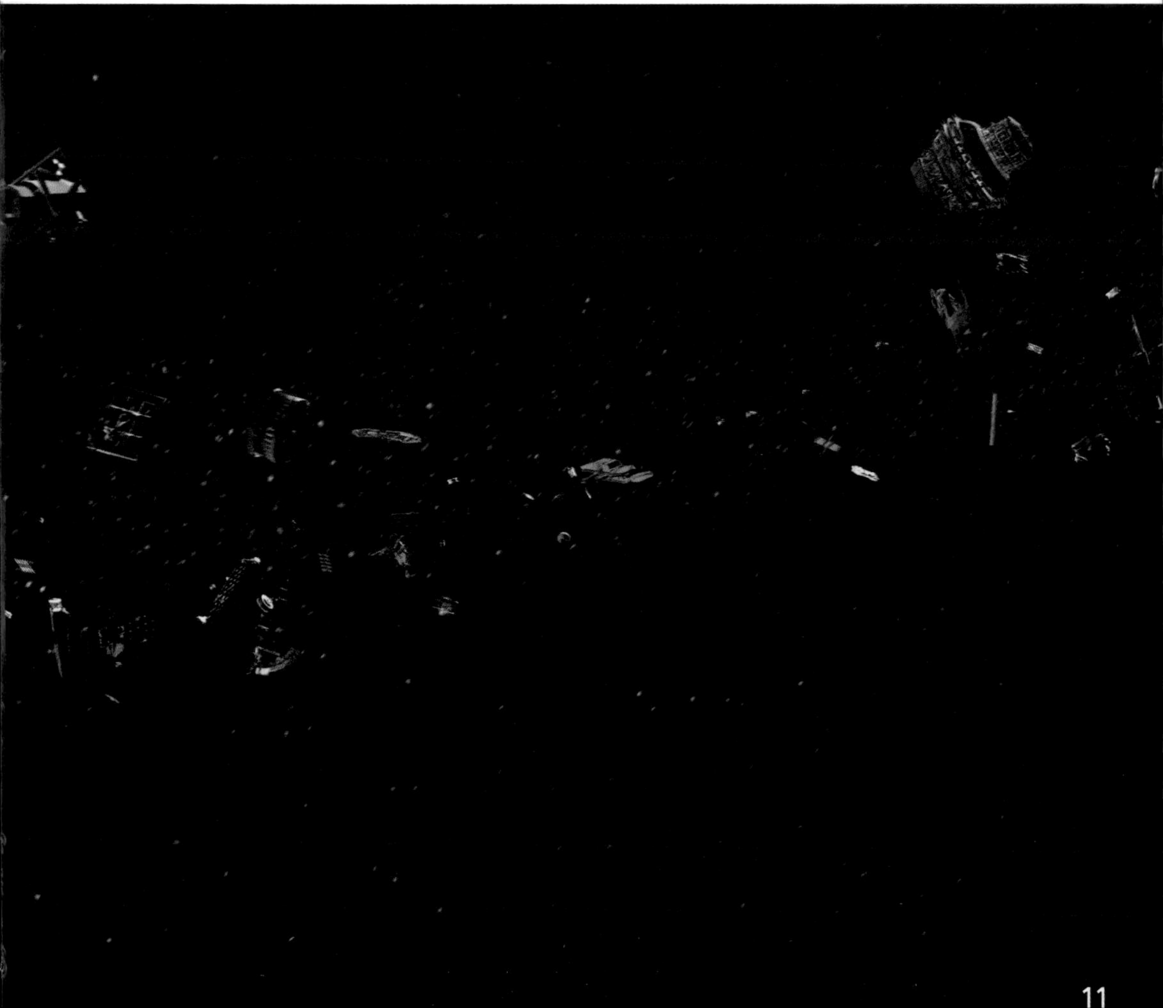

Space junk can crash into spacecrafts.

It can push other spacecraft off their **orbits**.

MAKE CONNECTIONS

Things in space orbit. They move in a circle. They move around objects with more gravity.

- How could space junk push spacecraft out of orbit?
- How could space junk create danger?

Orbits are paths spacecrafts travel on.

They are paths planets and other space-objects travel on.

Scientists **monitor** how much space junk orbits earth.

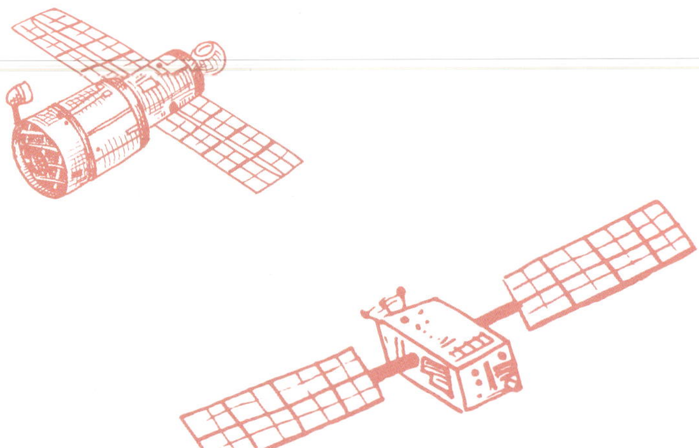

Monitor means watch carefully.

Scientists keep track of space junk bigger than a softball.

They inspect spacecraft that has returned to Earth.

They check to see what's missing.

Scientists are finding **innovative** ways to clean up space junk.

Innovative means new and inventive.

Scientists use special tools, such as lasers.

Lasers measure the distance of objects.

They hit the space junk in orbit. They bounce back to Earth.

Lasers only work at **twilight** but scientists are making new tools.

Twilight is a time of day. It is right before sunrise and right after sunset.

DECODE IT

The word *twilight* has 2 silent letters.

- Break it into chunks: twi-light.
- Both vowels sounds are long *i*.
- The letters *g* and *h* are silent. Long ago, they made a sound. Today, they make a long *i*.
- *Twilight* is pronounced TWIY-liyt.

PUT IT TOGETHER

Detail:
It can come from space and human-made objects.

Detail:
Scientists use lasers to clean up space junk. They are making new tools.

Main Idea:
Space junk is trash in space. It can be dangerous.

Detail:
It can come from spacecraft.

Detail:
Space junk can hit spacecraft, so scientists keep track of it.

Detail:
There are millions of pieces of space junk orbiting Earth. They move very fast.

LEARN MORE

BOOKS

Loh-Hagan, Virginia. *Introduction to Space*. Ann Arbor, MI: 45th Parallel Press, 2025.

Loh-Hagan, Virginia. *Weird Science: Space*. Ann Arbor, MI: 45th Parallel Press, 2022.

Tyson, Neil deGrasse. *StarTalk: Young Readers Edition*. Washington, DC: National Geographic Kids, 2018

ONLINE

Search these online sources with an adult:

- NASA | Games and Interactives
- NASA+ | Explore Topics

GLOSSARY

debris (duh-BREE) what is left when a thing breaks up; pieces of waste

innovative (IH-nuh-vay-tiv) new and inventive

monitor (MAH-nuh-tuhr) to watch carefully

orbits (OR-buhts) curved paths of objects around stars, planets, or moons

spacecraft (SPAYS-kraft) a vehicle used to travel into and through space

twilight (TWIY-liyt) time of day right before sunrise or right after sunset

vehicles (VEE-uh-kuhlz) things that carry people or other things

INDEX